Hear My Voice

REVEREND SHIRLEY GAMBLE

WESTBOW
PRESS®
A DIVISION OF THOMAS NELSON
& ZONDERVAN

This book is a work of non-fiction. Unless otherwise noted, the author and the publisher make no explicit guarantees as to the accuracy of the information contained in this book and in some cases, names of people and places have been altered to protect their privacy.

WestBow Press books may be ordered through booksellers or by contacting:

WestBow Press
A Division of Thomas Nelson & Zondervan
1663 Liberty Drive
Bloomington, IN 47403
www.westbowpress.com
844-714-3454

Scripture taken from the King James Version of the Bible.

ISBN: 978-1-6642-3561-8 (sc)
ISBN: 978-1-6642-3560-1 (e)

Print information available on the last page.

WestBow Press rev. date: 6/2/2021

To My Dear Michael

‿∞‿

When I thought there was no one I could share my life with, God sent you to me. A strong man with the smile of a little boy; so innocent and yet so powerful. You came with a light shining so bright that it would take us on a journey full of excitement and firsts. You Make life believable! My heart took wings and all my fears were lost in the joy of being your wife. You trust me with your life and I do the same for you. Thank you for allowing God to mold you and make you into a unique Man of God. If you catch me staring at you it is because your are awesome!

Contents

Introduction

I have always been a writer! In the fifth grade, my writing took me to the principal's office with my parents on two occasions. I didn't think the bus driver was aware of his unfair treatment of a young boy with a physical disability. I decided to make this injustice known to the principal in a letter. My father spoke in my defense, and asked "what's wrong with that", I was off the hook! The result of the second visit was not so positive because I addressed the unfairness of my teacher and the specifics were not good. My teacher had commented on my parents having a lot of children and not having any hobbies. At that age, I understood what she meant but it did not sit well with me. When the meeting ended and my parents and I were on the way home, my father said in his authoritative voice "this will not happen again."

I believe the reason I found confidence in writing was because it didn't require any talking. Things were going on in my head and I wanted them to be known but didn't know how to verbalize. I felt a person would remember more if it was written down.

My life has not been one of total ease nor oppression. Some of my dilemmas were self-created, some the result of allowing the wrong people to influence me. When I allowed God to be absent from my life, things didn't go so well. I was raised as a Christian young lady but decided to take a vacation from church when I left home. I am not bitter with God or any individual. I realize that in every situation, trial, and triumph I experienced, He allowed it to happen, and because He allowed it to happen He had a plan of escape and reason in mind. God never meant anything that happened in my life to kill me because I am still here. I give

Him honor, praise, and glory for allowing me to share a word of life and encouragement. I've had some good days, some bad days, some hills and valleys but I will not complain. I choose to accept all my life challenges and understand how they shaped my life. After all l have been through I still have joy.

My mission is to tell somebody to look up and live. As Christians, we read God's Word for guidance on how to live. You may not be faced with leading a group of people to cross the Red Sea or fight a Goliath but writers write to inspire you on how to deal with difficult day-to-day situations and how to praise God in every situation. We write so you can see that whatever you are going through is not unique to you. Revelation 12:11 says, And they overcame the devil by the blood of the Lamb and the word of their testimony, and they loved not their lives unto the death. I often wondered what it would be like to share your life experience, this is my first attempt. I speak from the heart those things that attributed to my relationship with my Lord and Savior Jesus Christ. I am not embarrassed about what I have been through. Someone needs to know that He is always there for you no matter how far you have strayed from Him. Because of my care and concern for others, my heart cries out on their behalf. So from my heart to yours, I say There is always hope!

Acknowledgments

I am eternally grateful to my husband Michael for the joy he brings me and the inspiration he gives me day to day, reminding me that I have so much to contribute to the world. God answered my prayers for a husband that I could talk to and enjoy no matter where we were. My prayers were answered with a sensitive, responsible, and Christian man. During two long deployments, Michael trusted me with house and home, finances, and raising two teenage children. He was able to focus on the mission of the United States Army and know that everything was well at home. When I received my Bachelor's Degree, he encouraged me to continue my education and receive my Master's degree. My prayer has always been that God would reveal our direction to Michael first and I would accept whatever he said. Amazingly, God will give me a thought and I say my prayer and off we go. I have no fear because my husband obeys God's direction.

I thank my parents John and Lula Schmidt, my seven siblings; John Jr, Claudette (Edward), Margaret, Alan, Patricia (Larry), Patrick, and Aaron. My nephew Jeremy who as a young child was an advisor to me. Thanks to my nephews, John III, and Eric, my niece Charmaine, uncles, aunts, and cousins. Thanks to my father and mother-in-law, brother-in-law, sister in law and her husband. To Dot, thank you for listening to God because we are still standing!

I give thanks to my Pastor, Harold H. Craig, Jr. MSMBC, Pastor Calvin Matthews, Isle of Patmos Baptist Church, Apostle Ernest James Arthur, Church of Transformation Full Gospel Baptist Church, and Pastor Hallie Tolbert, Westside Baptist Church. Thank you to the many men and women of God that inspired me and labored with me in the Gospel. I know the struggle of carrying the Word in your heart and sometimes being rejected and ignored. I owe thanks to the employees of the United States Postal Service in the different cities and states where we worked together. Thank you for trusting my leadership.

One

Three of Eight

In Genesis 17:1-4, God makes Abraham a promise that he would bless him: And when Abram was ninety years old and nine, the LORD appeared to Abram and said unto him, I am the Almighty God; walk before me and be thou perfect. 2 And I will make my covenant between me and thee and will multiply thee exceedingly. 3 And Abram fell on his face: and God talked with him, saying, 4 As for me, behold, my covenant is with thee, and thou shalt be a father of many nations.

I BELIEVE GOD had a conversation with John Schmidt, my father, and pointed out a wife for him that they would be a part of Abraham's promise. John Schmidt and Lula Hairston were united in matrimony and to their union, eight children were born. Eight unique personalities. Have to be honest, being the third child with a sibling born a year later put pressure on me. I felt as though I was being overlooked most of the time. I was always involved in some incident that resulted in discipline. I was the family entertainer and earned the name "Big Jane". My Halloween one-girl show was frequently requested by my siblings.

I often wonder how my father was able to provide for his family, he worked hard but only worked one job. He was active in church, read his bible, and applied discipline as needed. My mother was a homemaker and had childcare in the home. I was a grandpa's girl, I recall sitting with him in his hammock and listening to him talk about the things he was seeing and his thoughts about people. He was a Sunday School superintendent, very spiritual and I remember one of his favorite songs; "Yes God is real." You could feel his spirit and the church would get on fire.

The best gift parents can give their children is the introduction to Jesus Christ. Proverbs 22:6 says, train up a child in the way he should go and when he is old, he will not depart from it. Can you imagine raising eight children without knowing God? I don't think we would have survived if we had not been exposed to church in our early childhood. There were so many things that the church taught us; confidence in speaking, reading, and remembering Scripture and learning to respect our elders. We did our share of laughing and imitating the church mothers getting: "happy" in church.

There was somewhat of a written or unwritten rule that you could not be baptized until you were at least thirteen. There was a revivalist that came to preach every year; Rev. Jacob Dillard. He appeared to be about seven feet tall and he could PREEEECH. The year I became thirteen I was so excited about the opportunity to get baptized and start living a Christian life. I can tell young people that, peer pressure didn't come about in the 2000's it has always existed. I remember getting on the bus the Monday after baptism and some of the neighborhood girls called me a church girl. I think I was supposed to be angry with them but it was one of my proudest moments. Deciding to be baptized and accept Jesus Christ was the most important decision I made in life. I started feeling the Holy Spirit at an early age. There was a little closet in our bathroom that I would go in a read the bible while the rest of the family was doing other things.

I thank my parents for teaching us how to love each other and accept each other as individuals. When I think about the simple things we did as children I always smile. Eight children could think of a lot of ways to have fun. My grandfather had about twenty different fruit trees on his property. We would can apples and other fruits and always had some fruit to eat with dinner. The best apple tree happened to be in the family cemetery so we were afraid to go and pick them. Growing up none of us weighed much, maybe it was because of the fruit and the constant running around. We were taught to read and write before we went to school which made people consider us to be "very smart" We did have a little competition when it came to our school grades, everyone wanted to be on the top.

I used to watch my parents and listen to how they planned what they were going to do with us. We had family trips to Washington, D.C., Norfolk, Va, and Portsmouth, Va. On those trips, we had a lot of time to bond as a family and I am sure we got on our parent's nerves also. My first experience with eating crabs was in Norfolk where people ate them for every meal. I had no appetite for them at that time but I can put away some crabs now. There were simple things that we enjoyed like going to the Dairy Queen on Sunday evening to get a cone of ice cream. Those were the good old days! To this day my siblings like to get together although my family is the one outside of the area now. We practiced what our parents taught us, to love each other despite any differences and to make up quickly because family is all you have. It is a wonderful feeling to have brothers and sisters you can depend on.

Two

Walking in Your Purpose

Romans 8:28-30 .28 And we know that all things work together for good to those who love God, to those (A) who are the called according to His purpose. 29 For whom (B)He foreknew, (C)He also predestined (D)to be conformed to the image of His Son, (E)that He might be the firstborn among many brethren. 30 Moreover whom He predestined, these He also (F)called; whom He called, these He also (G)justified; and whom He justified, these He also (H)glorified. God calls us to service and work that you may influence others by the way you positively conduct yourself.

I DIDN'T FULLY understand how God was using me to change circumstances bigger than me. I remember being in class when the news came out that Dr. Martin Luther King had been assassinated. I had become a follower of his involvement in the civil rights movement. One thought in my mind was that if you became vocal about certain things you would be killed because President John Kennedy had also been assassinated. I lost some of my drive to be an excellent student. I loved to write and speak out in class. I began to take on a different attitude in school, I was quiet and reserved and kept to myself.

I was faced with the responsibility to do what God called me to do, I often asked what is my purpose, why am I here? I found my answer in Jeremiah 1:4-9 - Then the word of the Lord came unto me, saying,

> 5 Before I formed thee in the belly I knew thee, and before thou camest forth out of the womb I sanctified thee, and I ordained thee a prophet unto the nations.
>
> 6 Then said I, Ah, Lord God! behold, I cannot speak: for I am a child.
>
> 7 But the Lord said unto me, Say not, I am a child: for thou shalt go to all that I shall send thee, and whatsoever I command thee thou shalt speak.
>
> 8 Be not afraid of their faces: for I am with thee to deliver thee, saith the Lord.
>
> 9 Then the Lord put forth his hand and touched my mouth. And the Lord said unto me, Behold, I have put my words in thy mouth.

Walking – is a very important event in our lives. From the time we are born our parents are anticipating the moment, we will crawl, stand up and then walk on our own. Walking is a form of independence that everyone craves, to be mobile, go when and where you choose without relying on anyone else. It is not unusual for a person to say, wow I walked five miles last night and you will be eager to find out where they walked only to hear It was on a treadmill or an elliptical. These substitutes for real walking do not give you the visual pleasure of seeing the trees, birds, houses, and other people that are out walking. We have resorted to using our imagination about being in other places and experiencing other things and meeting new people.

What keeps you from walking in your purpose?

As Christians are you walking where we can encounter other people or has fear set in and we use the internet to meet people that are seeking other people but need to know Jesus Christ.

> Jeremiah 1: 7 - But the Lord said unto me, Say not, I am a child: for thou shalt go to all that I shall send thee, and whatsoever I command thee thou shalt speak.

One of the things that keep us from walking in our purpose is:

Not using our GPS – Are you referring to your global positioning system - GPS - a navigational system involving satellites and computers that can determine the latitude and longitude of a receiver on Earth by computing the time difference for signals from different satellites to reach the receiver. Some of the announcers have a name like Paula, Ann, and so forth and because of their unique voice, we tend to believe their instructions sometimes only to find ourselves in the wrong place.

There is One who has a foolproof GPS and that is God. God was the first to **introduce a GPS**:

The simple instructions for operating God's Positioning system can be found in:

> Proverbs 3:5-6:
>
> 5 Trust in the Lord with all thine heart; and lean not unto thine own understanding.
>
> 6 In all thy ways acknowledge him, and he shall direct thy paths.

Looking at other people is one of our biggest drawbacks in not appreciating who God made us. We are constantly plagued with trying to look like someone else, dress like someone else, and even talk like someone else and in the case of us ministers, sometimes we try to imitate other preachers.

Impatience – God called me so He must need me right now. There is no interest in preparation, studying, or growing in the word. Learn to Wait on the Lord:

1. Psalms 37:7-9 - Rest in the LORD, and wait patiently for him: fret not thyself because of him who prospereth in his way, because of the man who bringeth wicked devices to pass.
2. Psalms 37:34 - Wait on the LORD, and keep his way, and he shall exalt thee to inherit the land: when the wicked are cut off, thou shalt see [it].

Another deterrent to walking in our purpose is discouragement!

Galatians 6:9 - And let us not be weary in well doing: for in due season we shall reap if we faint not. Even if we face roadblocks, detours, and speed bumps it's okay because God has everything mapped out. I just want to encourage you today to walk in your purpose, I can't tell you what your purpose is but I do know if you begin to walk you will influence someone else along the way.

Finally, my brethren be strong in the Lord

Stay encouraged and know that you are on God's Positioning System (GPS) and you are right where he wants you. If you are finding it difficult to believe this it might be time for an upgrade in your system. To stay on course with the Global Positioning System, you must conduct some mandatory upgrades on the computer to identify the new construction and detours. To upgrade with God's GPS, some time spent on bended knees in prayer will give you the update you need. You might find out you are moving too fast or too slow. God has a destination in mind for us but a trip is no fun if you go alone.

When Jesus came to earth he was on a GPS – An angel received the satellite transmission and found Mary, they tracked Joseph and Mary from To the stable where he was born, to keep him from being killed he was tracked to the temple where he responded to the will his heavenly father had for him. Jesus studied the GPS plan until it was time for him to alter his directions, he had a special download of instructions when he was in the desert for 40 days and 40 nights, the GPS was updated and he was set on his course – destination Calvary. Jesus walked the earth and crowds followed him, they felt he was going in the right direction when the GPS identified water, He was placed on a boat where he could make GPS pointed out several attractions that Jesus needed to experience:

The blind man by the side of the road, the woman with the issue of blood, the demonic, the woman at the well, despite these attractions the GPS kept him on course. One day he stood before two men who were not friends until they met him and had to decide his fate. The GPS was uploaded and directed Jesus to a hill call calvary, there seemed to be a short in the system because his steps got slower and slower. once there was totally blackout and his GPS was out of service. The GPS declared – RECALCULATING, RECALCULATING, RECALCULATING, AND THE GPS LOST TRACK OF JESUS BUT EARLY SUNDAY MORNING AFTER THE SYSTEM REBOOTED – HE GOT UP!

Matthew 28:18-20 And Jesus came and spake unto them, saying, All power is given unto me in heaven and the earth. 19 Go ye therefore, and teach all nations, baptizing them in the name of the Father, and the Son, and the Holy Ghost: 20 Teaching them to observe all things whatsoever I have commanded you: and, lo, I am with you always, even unto the end of the world. Amen.

This is our purpose – Get a restart so you can walk in your purpose. We are to go out into the world and tell people of a living Savior who will direct us into truth and light. We are called to be the light of the world not hiding out and not taking the easy out of things. When it is necessary to speak against a situation it is our responsibility to use the wisdom and words of God to bring clarity.

Three

Be Yourself

Proverbs 22:6 Train up a child in the way he should go, and when he is old he will not depart from it. Proverbs 3:1 says my son, forget not my law, but let thine heart keep my commandments.

THERE ARE MANY opportunities in life to represent yourself with the values that have made and shaped you. You will be challenged to see how you respond to adversity and know if you have faith in God and trust Him to bring you out. When a young person is away from their parents and has God on their side, they will be able to make it. It is something how some of the things you resent being told become golden to you. You realize you have a repertoire of sayings and instructions to keep you from going wrong.

At age eighteen, I moved to Washington DC to live with a cousin and his family. I was alone in the big city. One of the things my father said about me was that I would have problems going there because I was too inexperienced. I had not been exposed to any worldly things to help me survive. I was determined to prove him wrong! The one scene I will always remember is the expression on my parent's faces when I boarded the Trailways bus going to Washington, D.C. It was hard to hold back the tears but I knew I had to make it. There were many weekends I spent crying and crying because I felt so lonely. After all, I went from a family of eight to be responsible for myself. My cousin was married with two children and the girls were young and kept me entertained until the day came when I had to move on my own. I recall walking in the snow trying to find an apartment and when I did I was so happy. There were many things I had to learn, like paying rent and not making a lot of noise at night. As much as I loved Shirley Caesar and Aretha Franklin, listening to them loudly late at night almost caused me to be evicted. Unfortunately, I had decided not to attend church when I first left home, I thought I knew enough to make it but an experience taught me otherwise.

I found a job working at a High's ice cream shop. You could tell me nothing; I was eighteen, had my apartment and a job in the big city! One day I was working and my older co-worker told me he had some business to attend to and I would be working by myself for a few hours. Not a problem! Three young men entered the store and immediately I felt danger. They walked around as if they were trying to decide what flavor of ice cream to purchase. I thought I would help them by saying "how may I help you?" One of the guys walked over to me and put a gun to my nose and said "you can help me by giving me all the money." I had been drilled on what to do if that should happen so I followed the instructions and they left quickly. I was so paralyzed I didn't know what to do. The co-worker returned and told me to call the police. I was grateful to be alive and I refused to allow this incident to cause me to get on a bus and go back to Virginia.

My cousin introduced me to a friend from Virginia that was in management at a bank, he interviewed me and I was hired on the spot. Yes, that little girl from Martinsville became a bank teller in Washington, D.C. I was now convinced that my decision to move away was ok. I would love to say that after that incident all was well with me but as it stands trouble seemed to come my way again.

Four

Chosen for Change

M Y EXPERIENCE OF being hired with the US Postal service was the most critical challenge I encountered. I was just a young intelligent black woman with a dream of working a "good job" to get the things I wanted. I passed the postal exam with a score of 99 out of a possible 100. I was hired by phone quickly. When I showed up at the Kensington post office I had the surprise of a lifetime. I waited almost an hour for the postmaster to come out and greet me on my first day. A secretary came out and told me there had been a mistake and there was no job available there. I began to "boil" and showed her my letter of employment for a clerk position, she disappeared again for over thirty minutes. At last, the postmaster came and told me that the only job they had was for a carrier, I told him I resigned from my job and it was already been filled so I will have to take it. He looked me in the eye and said, you can take it but I don't think you will be able to make it. From that day on I was tried and tested on every hand. As I began to ask questions about the post office and found they had never had a black employee and wasn't ready for me to be the one. My prayer life changed, I was praying all day long as I tried to work. I was reminded almost every day that I was black and I would not be there until the end of my probation. I read and recited different scriptures to myself, like Psalm 77: 1 I cried unto the Lord with my voice and he gave ear unto me. I could hear a voice telling me: don't be overwhelmed, I am right here. I know every step you take and the enemies that are working against. I had faith in God and I didn't argue with the people about anything they said to me. 1 Peter 3:11-14. let him eschew evil and do good, let him seek peace, and ensure it. For the eyes of the Lord are over the righteous and his ears are open unto their prayers but the face of the Lord is against them that do evil, And who is he that will harm you if ye be followers of that which is good.

I endured this hardship for almost ninety days which was the end of my probation I prayed and asked God to show me how to keep the job and He revealed some things to me. I needed to go and talk to someone about the mistreatment and I did. I was introduced to a Shop steward who informed me that he couldn't help me because I was black and the management would retaliate against him. I was advised to see an EEO counselor and file a complaint. I pursued it but when I talked with the representative, she didn't believe the things I said like, I was not permitted to park on the post office parking lot, sometimes I was only allowed to work one hour and sent home. I was delivering mail when a family let their Doberman pincer out and I was bitten all over and the supervisor would not get me any medical attention. I never received a paycheck because I wasn't processed to be hired. Thank God, the representative said she would make some surprise visits to the office and see what's happening. Fortunately the day she came out the supervisor was loud talking about a tv program and used an offensive term for black people. He kept repeating the word and said, Oh I forgot we have one of those here." I was really on the verge of losing my cool but kept reciting the scripture to myself. On that same morning, after working one hour, the supervisor told me to go home, we don't need you anymore today. Trust me when I say Anger opens the wrong door and I was about to go through it.

I was struggling to understand what I had done to deserve this situation. Was it because I was driven by the desire to make a lot of money not realizing that all success has its consequences. I remember hearing "MONEY IS THE ROOT OF ALL EVIL BUT THE SCRIPTURE SAYS IN 1 TIMOTHY 6:10, FOR THE LOVE OF MONEY, IS THE ROOT OF ALL EVIL. The love of money is the root of all evil. which while some coveted after, they have erred from the faith and pierced themselves through with many sorrows. I believe at this time I was loving money but I wasn't even getting paid. If I had not built a little savings I would not have been able to get to the job.

Once the EEO investigation was completed I was able to save my job although the postmaster planned to say I did not perform well enough to keep it. I was asked what I wanted as a resolution and asked to be transferred. I was transferred to another post office in Maryland. I knew this was a miracle from God because truly what the devil meant for evil He used it for my good, (Genesis 50:20-21)

I made a decision to release myself from the feelings I had of vengeance and resentment toward the perpetrators that almost took my sanity. I needed to be like Jesus! After he had risen from the dead and met with his disciples and told them about forgiveness: John 20:**19** On the evening of that first day of the week, when the disciples were together, with the doors locked for fear of the Jewish leaders, Jesus came and stood among them and said, "Peace be with you!" **20** After he said this, he showed them his hands and side. The disciples were overjoyed when they saw the Lord. **21** Again Jesus said, "Peace be with you! As the Father has sent me, I am sending you." **22** And with that he breathed on them and said, "Receive the Holy Spirit. **23** If you forgive anyone's sins, their sins are forgiven; if you do not forgive them, they are not forgiven."

If Jesus could forgive men for what they did to Him, surely I could. It took some time but I can say that forgiveness prevailed and my mind is free. I hope this will encourage someone to forgive a person that you know you need to forgive. If you believe in the Word you will realize that you're withholding your forgiveness. We should ask for forgiveness daily for ourselves and those we come in contact with. Unsettled issues will manifest themselves in anger, illness, and mental issues.

Five

The Fruit of the Spirit

Galatians 5: 22 But the fruit of the Spirit is love, joy, peace, longsuffering, kindness, goodness, faithfulness, gentleness, self-control.

T HINGS ARE NOT always what they appear to be. Sometimes what we see is a mirage, like a man on a desert praying for water, he sees his own shadow and thinks it is a waterfall. As he reaches out the only thing he can feel is the hot dry air.

As Christians, we are called to be recognized as children of God, not just in words but in our actions toward others. We exhibit these qualities only through the strengthening of the Holy Spirit in us.

To most people fruit is equated to something sweet and juicy. The fruit described in Galatians 5:22 is given to us by the Holy Spirit. If you can visualize a fruit bowl you can ascribe a piece of fruit to each of the nine attributes mentioned. Love is an apple, big, bright full, looks good on the outside, and once bitten can be very fulfilling. There is a crunch in the apple followed by a flow of sweet juice. When people meet us they are looking for the inside of us to match the outside appearance. A deeper acquaintance with us should not be disappointing and leave a sour taste in the other person's mouth.

Joy -grapes the more you eat the better you feel. There is a saying that life is not always like a bowl of cherries but give me a bowl of cherries and I will be very happy. The fruit of the spirit represents positive aspects of life. This is what it takes to make us successful and respect others. When we overlook our selfish desires and seek the happiness of someone else. Grapes represent an opportunity to share some of our experiences and our abundance with others.

Peace is a heartfelt desire of most people. There is nothing better than being able to rise early in the morning and appreciate the beautiful nature God has given us. Spending a day in relaxation no frets, no fears, anxiety, or anger.

Long-suffering - oranges Patience with yourself and those around you. We must be patient with God; He is always working but we are not able to see it with our natural eyes. We must be steadfast in our faith and wait on God to act on our behalf. In addition to waiting we should not have a complaining spirit. Spending more time in prayer and thanksgiving will help us with this. 1 Corinthians 15:58 says therefor my beloved brethren, be ye steadfast unmovable, always abounding in the work of the Lord for as much as ye now that your labor is not in vain in the Lord we must not give up on doing good when things do seem fair. Like the orange, we may get shipped from place to place, be bruised, squeezed, put in extreme heat and cold. When they arrive at their final destination they are examined and set out for our enjoyment.

Like the orange, it may take some time for us to arrive at the place God wants us to be. If we set our hearts on making it and not giving up we will get there.

Kindness - Kiwi fruit As you travel the area you may see signs in the neighborhood that say " Be Kind": Two young sisters in LaGrange Kentucky started the project of making these signs and donated the proceeds to local charities in their area. Being kind can be as good for your well-being as a kiki. The fruit offers vitamin C and other antioxidants if eaten daily have great benefits to the body. A daily dose of kindness is good for the soul and to those shown it as well. Ephesians 4:32 - And be ye kind one to another, tenderhearted, forgiving one another even as God for Christ's sake hath forgiven you.

Goodness - blueberries are rich in benefits to the brain, heart, and blood sugar. When we extend goodness toward others it helps their thinking and the heart is warmed. Galatians 6:10, so then as we have the opportunity, let us do what is good toward all men, and especially toward those who are of the household of faith. It shouldn't be difficult to honor and respect those that share the same faith as you do. Sometimes we can be judgemental of others and forget that how we treat them affects the way they think and may also break their heart. Just a few blueberries can satisfy the taste for something sweet, so a few kind words can do the same.

Faithfulness - strawberries with good planting situation, strawberries can produce. They are easy to reproduce and are grown all around the country and the world. Uses desserts, in a bowl they will be a good satisfying treat. Strawberries lower cholesterol, are sodium and fat-free, and high in antioxidants. Needless to say, they are anti-aging fruit. This fruit relates to faithfulness because of its consistent qualities and uses on a long-term basis. Hebrews 10:23, Let us hold fast the confession of our hope without wavering for he who promised is faithful.

Gentleness - Pears are a good representation of how we should treat one another. Pears bruise easily. They can grow and thrive in cold and wet climates, can survive heat and cold. This is how we interact with others, hot sometimes and cold sometimes but expect to be received anyhow. Gentleness comes from a state of humility. To be gentle we must not view ourselves as better than someone else. A person showing gentleness can help that same person that mistreated them. Sometimes gentleness can be perceived as a weakness, however, it exhibits great strength. Hebrews 13:1-2 - Keep on loving one another as brothers and sisters. Do not forget to show hospitality to strangers, for by doing some people have shown hospitality to angels without knowing it.

Self-control- promote good cholesterol with blackberry fiber. Blueberries are full of antioxidants and lower the risk of heart disease and cancer. They offer other health benefits such as anti-inflammatory. Blueberries are often called Super Food. Self-control can be compared with blueberries because they help to monitor health concerns and offer strength and energy for physical endurance. Self-control is the ability to keep your disruptive emotions ad impulses in check. The same way blueberries prevent certain diseases, Self control prevents us from emotional outbursts and disruptions. Psalm 141:3-4 - Set a watch oh Lord before my mouth, keep the door of your lips, incline not my heart to any evil thing, to practice wicked works with me that work iniquity and let me not eat of their dainties. James 1:19 -Wherefore, my beloved brethren, let every man be swift to hear, slow to speak, slow to wrath.

Six

Smile anyhow

ONE OF MY favorite phrases is: I am glad we don't look like what we've been through!

On several occasions when I was asked to do the call to worship in our service I would say this to engage the congregation: Look at your neighbor on your left and say, you know what, you look good today, now look to the person on your right and say you know what you sure look good today., now look in your s spiritual mirror and say You sure look good today, I am so glad I don't look like what I've been through. I cannot begin to tell you how many times I have had to stand, do my normal duties, go to work, and all when my spirit was on E and it would have taken more than a full gas station to get me off the floor.

Philippians 4:8 - Finally, brethren, whatsoever things are true, whatsoever things are honest, whatsoever things are just, whatsoever things are pure, whatsoever things are lovely, whatsoever things are of good report; if there be any virtue, and if there be any praise, think on these things.

Sitting in class one day a student began singing a song by Stevie Wonder titled Lately. The song said lately I've been staring in the mirror, very slowly picking me apart trying to tell myself I have no reason with your heart." Sometimes we can allow our thoughts to take us someplace that is not positive or have a reason to be a part of our minds. There is always something good to think about. God gave us a brilliant mind which allows us to take strolls in our past which had hidden treasures that brought smiles, laughter, and sometimes tears. Do you recall some days from your childhood when all you thought about was having fun, playing with dolls, watching cartoons, and buying penny candy from the corner store?

During one of my husband's deployments, I tell you I think I lost a little bit of my mind. I was working full time, running the house, trying to keep the children in check but I was unable to sleep at night. At most I would sleep about four hours, tossing, turning, and thinking. The thoughts that came to my mind were mostly negative. When I did sleep I had a repetitive dream that I was walking toward what was supposed to be my husband's casket but he was never there. After that, I didn't care if I slept or not because the feeling was terrible. I had to regroup- I started fasting and praying more. The children and I would sit on the floor late at night and watch a tele-evangelist together and began to feel some relief.

One of the things I remember most is that people didn't reach out to us or include us in things, perhaps because they didn't know if we would be sad or withdrawn and spoil their fun. We filled our time with long rides on Saturday, eating and shopping. We were active in our church and I was on the Praise Team which kept me very busy.

My Pastor, Arthur made sure I stayed involved in church. As I was looking through music I found a song that expressed my feelings and I listened to it on repeat and cried all night long. The song was Falling in Love with Jesus. I told God I would introduce this song to my husband when he returned from Iraq and we could sing it as a duet. I held the song in my heart for over nine months before his return. I started to smile again because I had a "secret", a song Jesus had given me. The song became an anthem for us. I remember singing it at the funeral of a five-year-old boy that drowned, we didn't know him but his family needed support. I believe someone was saved that day. We sang it at the funeral of our First Lady Arthur and the funeral of my father. That was a day I needed a smile and I believe he was pleased with our tribute.

Sometimes we can become so self-absorbed we don't realize someone around us needs a smile. Try on your worse day to seek out someone that appears to need a smile and give them one of yours. You can believe they will smile back. Why smile? Smiling creates an atmosphere of calmness and. Once you give in to a smile the next thing is a contagious laugh. It is very difficult to think about anything negative when you are engaged in laughter.

Proverbs 17:22 says a merry heart is good medicine, but a crushed heart dries up the bones. When there is a situation that you cannot do anything about, it is best to trust God and accept it as is. Everything is temporary and we learn how to handle things without falling apart. As we become wiser we can see the outcome of some situations before they develop. If that be the case we learn to walk away from what we know will not be good for us. There is a reason for everything and God is leading and directing us in all situations if we allow Him to do so.

Isaiah 26:3 Thou wilt keep him in perfect peace whose mind is stayed on thee: because he trusteth in thee.

Seven

Trusting God

Psalm 31:1, In thee O Lord I put my trust, let me not be ashamed: deliver me in thy righteousness.

Matthew 6:33, Seek ye first the kingdom of God and his righteousness and all these things will be added unto you. Growing up in the church I learned many things about life, how to treat others, honor your parents, elders, live honestly and all.

I DON'T RECALL hearing about tithing until I joined a church in Washington D.C and giving was explained in the terms of more than paying dues and giving an offering. This happened at a time in my life when I wanted more, I was working and making money but I wanted to get out of the apartments in DC and buy a house. I also needed a car for the job that I needed that would help me get those things. I took this new information and I told God I will do this type of giving and I BELIEVE your word is true. I began to read everything I could about giving, tithing, and blessings from God. It was like a whole new world had opened before me. I read every scripture I could find until I was overjoyed about the principle of giving.

Some Christians pretend they don't want money or finer things in life. I concluded that it is because they don't want to follow the instructions of God on how to achieve them. Yes, it originated in the Old Testament but it is truly relevant for current day living. God doesn't want to limit us or He would not have included it in His Word. In Joshua 1:8 God told Joshua, this book of the law shall not depart out of thy mouth; but thou shalt meditate therein day and night, that thou mayest observe to do according to all that is written therein. for then shalt thou shall make thy way prosperous and then thou shalt have good success. I wanted to please God in this area of my life and he blessed me. In one year I bought a house and a new car, paid my tithes faithfully, and had a few dollars in the bank.

There was one other area in my life that I desired to be fulfilled. I had a desire to be married. I had a lot to learn about love. I saw a perfect example of a husband and wife in my parents. I didn't realize there was a lot of work put into a relationship that would lead to a good marriage. I was looking around and thinking I was supposed to find this person. I realized if I read about tithing in the bible God must have something to say about marriage. Thank God for the concordance in the Bible. I found lots of scriptures and began to read other books. I read about what a woman should be like in Titus 2:5 - women should be discreet, chaste, keepers at home, good, obedient to their own husbands, that the word of God be not blasphemed. I thought I can do that I had seen it before. I started thinking back about how my parents operated. There were a lot of people getting married and I was invited to some weddings. I was overwhelmed with the pretty dresses and nice-looking men in suits. If I had to be honest I would say satan was probably laughing at me saying; that fool is in for a surprise.

I started meeting young men but I didn't know how to talk to them because this was new to me. Of course, I ran into the issue of sex, and I would quickly tell them I had to be married before having sex. This didn't sit too well with the guys and one person told me that I would probably never get married so I may as well do it. I cried at those words but I had decided to trust God. God wants to be involved in every aspect of your life. It is impossible to have a good relationship without God in it.

When God has a mission for us, he does not leave us alone. We should be able to rely on our past experiences with him and do not give up in the middle of the storm. There is a point in a storm when things change. If we listen to His instructions we will not lose our life. We may encounter rough times and sometimes it seems there is no hope but don't jump ship, help is on the way! At times in our lives situations and circumstances cause us to feel overwhelmed, abandoned, and much like Paul in this scripture; shipwrecked. We may feel that everyone around us is against us and there is no hope in sight. As we begin to release ourselves from self-pity and pride we can see that we are not in this "boat" by ourselves. Others have as many issues and concerns as we do. We must learn to reach out and help rescue someone else. When we take our eyes off ourselves we can see the beauty of life.

Would you agree - When we lose sight of God every incident, not to our liking becomes a storm, contrasted and compared to the physical storms of life? A disobedient child is like a tornado, a wayward spouse is compared to a hurricane, taking off and leaving a trail of destruction a Godless Boss is like a volcano, erupting at any given time. Don't be overcome by your storm, trust in Jesus who calms every storm, but we have to call Him. We can have the midnight in our storms when Jesus shows up. It is never too late to trust Him.

When people around us see how we handle our storms, they are either encouraged and trust God or they feel we are just saying that we believe and trust God only when things are going our way. If you have friends or loved ones that don't read the Bible, they are reading you and your response to life.

Eight

God made me special

Psalm 139:14 - I will praise thee for I am fearfully and wonderfully made, marvelous are thy works; and that my soul knoweth right well.

I AM A controller, I have a CPU, motherboard, hard drive, RAM, graphic card, power supply all the makings of a computer. God gave Adam all these things when he created him. I almost lost it all when Adam and Eve blew it in the garden. It took only one instance of not following instructions to lose it. God gave us a second chance!

God wrote the script for my operating system and it is perfectly coded. He established the times for updating my system and deleting old files; the things that find their way in my life but have no purpose. Like Psalm 23:4: he restores me to my default position so I can walk through the valley of the shadow of death and reach my destiny even if I have to close my eyes. I get to retrieve lost things as I find my way through and I get to see the things that are left behind on purpose.

God reminds me that as long as I am plugged into His power supply there is nothing I cannot accomplish. Philippians 4:13 I can do all things through Christ which strengtheneth me. As I follow the path God set for me, He expects me to follow the instructions outlined in the owner's manual. My bible, sixty six books of words from God. Any scenario of life is addressed in these books. From the beginning of my life until the end I can see what I could encounter and find the solution also.

Deleted files: He promises that those things and people that are not for my good will be cast away from me. Philippians 3:13 Brethren, I count not myself to have apprehended: but this one thing I do, forgetting those things which are behind, and reaching forth unto those things which are before,

I receive my daily updates when I start my day with prayer. Listening to God allows me to know which direction to follow and how to spend my day. Like a computer, He may want me to restart so I can get the updated information.

He gives me time to recover by ending my day with rest and sleep. When I refresh I can do more, understand more, and see a little further ahead. I can anticipate what will work best in a situation better than if I am tired. God designed us according to our predestination. I often wondered why people have unique features and what are to be used for. I can use myself as an example; high cheekbones, almond eyes, small wide lips, long legs, thin wrists which tell me I was not intended to be a very weighty person. I have an unusual sense of humor and I see God in everything or situation I encounter. In writing this book I feel his hand directing me on the keyboard. The thoughts are being dictated by Him; I am just moving my fingers.

My husband and I were riding along and saw an old historic building. It appeared to need some tender loving care; tall bushes and peeling paint were obvious. My thought was, I am glad God made me special not like a man builds a house. Houses deteriorate, walls cave in, the roof falls in, windows break out, basements flood, and cave in. Appliances in the house break down and have to be replaced. Electrical wiring becomes faulty, pipes rust, and major heating and air systems stop working. As for me, my body is built to last a lifetime. My brain, my mind; my operating system is maintained and need regular checkups. God gave men wisdom to invent comparable items to sustain my statue and my health. Sometimes my body parts show signs of wearing out and need so help. There are specialists able to order replacement organs, cosmetics, dentistry, hair growth, and vitamins and minerals to aid in improving. What God made He can sustain!

Many buildings have been constructed and demolished. Many cars have been built and deteriorated. I am still standing with a few upgrades. Standing to show that God is marvelous and I am His handiwork, ever living and breathing until He says the word.

Nine

Where to find God

B E STILL AND know that I am God, Psalm 46:10 Every day begin your day with a thank you and praise. Oh Lord, our Lord how excellent is thy name in all the earth. How you love me and care for me even when I don't seem to care for myself. You watch over me when I sleep and whisper in my ear to say it is time to rise up. My heart rises knowing that you have me for the rest of the day. I need you this day to show me where to spend my time, is there someone that needs me today? Please anoint my eyes that I may see who it is and be able to give them what they need. Let the strings of my heart play a melody in someone's life today that the tears they carrying will not fall upon their cheeks today but a smile will adorn their face. Be the light that guides me to that place where you wait for me.

Psalms 91:1-16 - He that dwelleth in the secret place of the Most High shall abide under the shadow of the Almighty. To appreciate God and His presence we need to steal away to a place when we can only hear his voice. There should be some time each day when you sit in a quiet place without music, tv and other distractions, I tell you that His spirit will fill the room. Jesus often took time to be with His Father, to reflect to rejuvenate, cry out, and to get instructions. He invited his disciples to join him in prayer in the garden but they fell asleep. Even when He prayed longer than he thought and came back to let them know but they were still asleep. What if you fall asleep while praying? I have a vision of Jesus patting me on my head and assuring me everything will be alright. I find rest in Him, not worried or concerned with what is going on around me.

Matthew 26:36-56 Jesus was a consistent prayer and He was not particular about where He prayed. When He needed to talk to His Father it was the time and place to pray. You can find God in prayer, in praise, and in worship. Psalm 34:4 says I sought the Lord, and He heard me, and delivered me from all my fears.

Psalm 103:1, one of my favorite scriptures: Bless the Lord Oh my soul and all that is within me, bless His holy name. Often recovering from a feeling of emptiness and defeat I found comfort in letting God know that I desired to give Him my all. It is in this time of praise that I could feel the Spirit rising within me I wanted to cry out in my loudest voice from the depth of my soul, knowing that without Him I am nothing but with Him I am everything.

You can find God in the trees, the wind, the water, the birds, and their melodious tunes. God has given all His creation a voice to praise Him with. The birds make perfect melody without attending choir rehearsals. The trees bend and bow as God's special praise dancers. The waters flow, rise, and fall with the command of God's voice.

The closer you get to God you can begin to speak in his Holy language. I dare you to try this because once you have the experience of speaking in tongues you will desire it but it cannot be practiced or prompted. You must carry yourself in such a way that the Holy Spirit dwells in you and wants to use you. Allow yourself to rest in and cry out to Him from the depths of your soul, no regard to outside sounds, just let Him come into your space.

God is omnipresent He is present everywhere with His whole Being at all times. God is spirit; He has no physical form. He is present everywhere in that everything is immediate in His presence. At the same time, He is present everywhere in the universe. No one can hide from Him and nothing escapes His notice.

Ten

Expectation Wanting More!

G OD WANTS MORE for us! He presented us with a formula for receiving everything we desire. Matthew 21:22 And all things, whatsoever ye shall ask in prayer, believing, ye shall receive." The key is believing in Him! It's alright to have self-confidence, however; without God, we can do nothing. With Him, we can do all things through his strength that works in us.

My desire for more must not override God's will for my life. When I say I believe in Him, I take on His character and patience becomes my name. Jesus came to the earth knowing that His stay was temporary. He did not do anything to rush his departure to go back to His father. He was walking out his destiny, every step that He took. He could have used some power on His own and say that He was responsible for the creation. Jesus honored HIs father to the point of saying that the only words he spoke were the words the Father told Him to say

For some reason, we do not want to get older except when we are going from fifteen to sixteen or twenty - twenty one. Growing older as a Christian our desire should be to draw closer to God. We have done foolish things and repented and seeing that our life should be an example to someone else. As we become part of the retirement community our desire to have something to show for our years of labor and "a little something" put away for ourselves and our family. We begin to realize that we need to give more of ourselves to God, to allow Him to work in our lives. Our belief and hope in miracles increase because health issues arise. We don't want any disease or ailment that will cause us not to enjoy our "golden years."

It is honorable to desire more, but you must do more. You can achieve more when you share with others. As you share you multiply yourself and that becomes more. Sometimes we take our eyes off Jesus and think we have time to come back to him after we have run after a dream that often becomes a nightmare. In Matthew 6:33, Jesus gives more instructions on success; Seek ye first the kingdom of God and all these things will be added unto you. He warns us about worrying about food and clothes and cars and houses. He points out if we observe nature and the little animals how he provided for their every need. The more he will do for us, we can trust Him to do it.

In the last days, I will pour out my Spirit on all flesh this scripture was written in Joel 2:28 and repeated in Acts 2:25-30. For those who think the Old Testament was only for the olden days, God had to repeat himself in the New Testament. Acts 2:25 And I will restore to you the years that the locust hath eaten, the cankerworm, and the caterpillar, and the palmerworm, my great army which I sent among you.**26** And ye shall eat in plenty, and be satisfied, and praise the name of the LORD your God, that hath dealt wondrously with you: and my people shall never be ashamed.**27** And ye shall know that I am in the midst of Israel and that I am the LORD your God, and none else: and my people shall never be ashamed.

28 And it shall come to pass afterward, that I will pour out my spirit upon all flesh; and your sons and your daughters shall prophesy, your old men shall dream dreams, your young men shall see visions:**29** And also upon the servants and upon the handmaids in those days will I pour out my spirit.**30** And I will shew wonders in the heavens and the earth, blood, and fire, and pillars of smoke. **31** The sun shall be turned into darkness, and the moon into blood, before the great and terrible day of the LORD come.**32** And it shall come to pass, that whosoever shall call on the name of the LORD shall be delivered: for in mount Zion and in Jerusalem shall be deliverance, as the LORD hath said, and in the remnant whom the LORD shall call.

Eleven

Seasons

A T THIS MOMENT we are in a pandemic which is a season of uncertainty. I pray that when you read this book that season will be over. My hands are tied, my ears and heart are open, love is overflowing. Past disappointments have disappeared. There is not much to do because of the mandate for social distancing and limited participation in activities. Working from home has been a true blessing. I had become weary of driving to work every day and being away from home. When I find myself in a disturbing mood, only my husband can tell. This has been an opportunity to draw closer to each other. Being together twenty-four seven has been wonderful; we have developed a unique way to attend to each other's needs differently than before. While working outside the home, I would wonder how he is doing in his office, is he taking the time to drink enough water or taking a break from sitting all day. Now I get to ask him if he would like some water or something to eat and still do my daily work.

God gave us four seasons: Winter Spring Summer and Fall. Ecclesiastes 3:1 -To everything there is a season, and a time for every purpose under the sun. It is said that living in one season would not be fruitful because everything needs time to grow and a time to rest. I am not a fan of winter because it seems to slow me down. I am not motivated by cold weather because it makes me want to stay in hiding and not get out in the open. If there is such thing as hibernating like a bear that describes how I feel. The sun doesn't shine a lot in the winter and I need the sun to warm me and help me see the wings of angels in the sky. If it rains in winter, it is cold and depressing. I could stay in the house and never go out. There is a form of depression called Seasonal Affective Disorder also known as SAD or winter depression. Although this is a recognized disorder, I realize I have been doing the opposite of how to avoid entering a depressed state. The effective ways to handle the disorder include making your environment sunnier and brighter, get outside take walks to eat in the park sit in the sun when it is out. Reading and meditating on God's word is a good remedy for this.

God uses winter to allow the earth to rest from growing crops and regenerating or rejuvenating itself for another season. It is a time of rest. I do get rest in winter because I am not inclined to do much. He sends the snow and sleet to moisturize the earth and prepare it for the next season. God tries to give us rest but too often we try to crowd our lives with so many things of which most are not worthy of our time. Why can't I just sit down, close my eyes and take a breath sometimes?

Spring is a time of encouragement for me, I gather myself to begin an activity that I have avoided. We plant bulbs, into the ground they go and we don't know what's going on. It enters a Season of Silence There is a time to be quiet so you can hear from God.

Proverbs 17:27-28. 27 The one who has knowledge uses words with restraint, and whoever has understanding is even-tempered. 28 Even fools are thought wise if they keep silent, and discerning if they hold their tongue.

Stop Talking, that is an impossible request that many people should honor. We live in a world that makes silence uncomfortable. Sometimes we find ourselves wanting to take to the streets with a bull horn and declare that the world has gone mad. Or we get some tidbit of information and believe everyone needs to know about it. Social media has become a major platform for transmitting information whether true or false. For many people, social media has become their lifeline for communication with family and friends. Often the response of the so-called friends can cause heartbreak and disappointment.

In the Book of Luke, Chapter 1, Priest Zacharias experienced a season of silence. He and the congregation came before God I prayed for a son. He was married to Elisabeth, daughter of Aaron. She was barren and they were both up in age and it seemed impossible that they could have a child. In verse 13, But the angel said unto him, Fear not Zacharias; for thy prayer is heard, and thy wife Elisabeth shall bear thee a son, and thou shall call his name John. And thou shalt have joy and gladness, and many shall rejoice at his birth. For he shall be great in the sight of the Lord, and shall drink neither wine nor strong drink; and he shall be filled with the Holy Ghost, even from his mother's womb. Zacharias challenged the angel's words by asking; how will I know this since I am an old man and my wife well stricken in years. And the angel said to him I am Gabriel, that stand in the presence of God, and am sent to speak unto thee, and to shew thee these glad tidings. And behold, thou shalt be dumb and not able to speak, until the day that these things shall be performed, because thou believest not my words, which shall be fulfilled in their season. This began Zacharias' season of silence because of his unbelief. As the angel Gabriel told him, he was unable to speak until eight days after his son was born. The child was being present for the ritual of circumcision and the people called out his name as Zacharias but his mother Elisabeth spoke up and said his name is John. It was customary to name a boy child after his father. This controversy required a response from the father. Zacharias asked for a writing tablet to clear the situation up and began to write his name as "John", immediately his tongue was loosed and he was able to speak.

Choose Your Words Wisely – Talk with a purpose, accomplish something good with your words. Listen – We are all guilty of having conversations in which we are 'halfway listening' meaning …My opinion without facts is of no value to me or anyone else. When asked your opinion of a particular situation we must be careful because self can respond and harm another person while silence can render objectivity. Don't React – Silence can be an incredible gift amid conflict. Whether you are …Listening is so important and it is difficult to talk and listen at the same time. This is a reason for so many confusing relationships.

Season of prayer - 2 Chronicles 7:14 If my people which are called by my name would humble themselves and pray, seek my face, turn from their wicked ways, then will I hear from heaven, I will forgive their sins and heal their land. A time for self-evaluation, not finger-pointing. We have all sinned and fallen short of the word. We ask how do we have the responsibility of praying and perpetrators continuing to sin, kill and steal and not acknowledge God.

Our prayers are weapons of mass destruction. As we aim our thoughts and hands toward heaven we can ignite a force that changes things and people. When we add God to the equation it like a bomber using TNT to destroy a building. When we pray we are crushing and destroying evil thoughts and actions. Vengeance is mine saith the Lord (Romans 12:19), all we need to do is bring our petitions before him.

Season of summer, everything is out in the open, there is freedom in the air, less clothing to wear. Summer how I have longed for you! Sitting by my window in my home office watching the barrenness of the field. It looks so cold and lonely, nothing stirring except an occasional vulture seeking food. When I think of you I want to turn off my space heater and run outside for the full feeling of the sun. I can't wait to feel the sun on my head, my arms, and my legs. I will get to the beach and run to the water and get sand in between my toes. I don't think summer gets its fair share of time at least not for me!

Twelve

The best is coming –

THERE IS SOMEONE in the teens, 20s 30s 40s 50s 60s 70s 80s, and 90s that need to know that as long as you are still living there is a purpose for your life and the best is yet to come. The Lord promises His continuous love and concern for the elderly. "I will be your God throughout your lifetime -- until your hair is white with age (Isaiah 46:4-6).

It is never too late to make your life count. I read about an 80-year-old person graduating from college. Even more, intriguing a 103-year-old man skydiving on his birthday.

All that we do should be an encouragement to someone else and not discouragement. I recall once asking God – What am I here for, it was at a moment when I was disappointed about the plans I had for myself and pushed to do things without getting his approval. These acts of "doing my own thing or doing it my way' cost me my joy. I was feeling so low I thought things would be better if I didn't exist. One night I was so fed up with myself that I went to bed crying, asking God to take me. I wasn't interested in taking any pills or jumping off a building, I wanted a quiet exit from all my pain. When I woke up the next day, I couldn't believe I was still alive. I began to cry out to God for help, to show me what to do. Hear my, prayer, O Lord, and let my cry come unto thee.(Psalm 102:1)

My life was never the same, my eyes were opened to the people and things around me. I realized I didn't have to allow people to control me or accept their negative treatment toward me. I learned to accept being alone, a single person. I started looking at every aspect of my life and how I could improve things. My bible became my best friend and my road map.

I will say that there are different periods in life where we see life differently. In the twenties, it's all about freedom from parents and being able to live and enjoy life; have all the fun you can! We meet new people and learn about new things, some of which we would be better off not knowing. We discover the opposite sex and either find interest in them or dislike them. I recall it being a little scary meeting young men from different places and not knowing who to trust. Fortunately, I was with two of my sisters in my twenties so I had someone I could talk to and not feel isolated. I had some other friends but they didn't think as I did. The worse advice you can receive is from someone in the same age group as you and neither of you have any experience in life.

Then there was the big push to get married before thirty. Unfortunately, some people have not reached an understanding of what marriage entails. It is much more than wearing a beautiful dress and moving to a new house.

Scripture - Behold I will do a new thing!(Isaiah 43:19) What does new look like to you, is it something you've never heard or seen or imagined? No matter how much we think we know or desire fear is dread. 1 Corinthians 2:9 says But it is written, eye hath not seen, nor ear heard, neither have entered into the heart of man, the things which God hath prepared for them that love Him.

Fear plays an important role in creating an atmosphere of "Best". The word IF comes into play in moving forward with ideas. Some of the best work can be done in the realm of fear. The bible tells us Fear not for I am with you, be not dismayed for I am your God. I will strengthen you. Yes, I will help you, I will uphold you with my righteous right hand. Isaiah 41:10. Fear is dismay, alarm and panic. Fear can be overcome by taking action.

Best is coming when Jesus returns. Mark 13:32 says But about that day or hour no one knows, not even the angels in heaven, nor the Son but only the Father. Some ask why is He taking so long? Jesus is patiently waiting to come back because he is giving humanity as much time as possible to choose to follow him. Jesus wants as many people as possible to repent and return to heaven with Him.

Joel 2:12-13, 12 Even now," declares the LORD, "return to me with all your heart, with fasting and weeping and mourning." 13 Rend your heart and not your garments. Return to the LORD your God, for he is gracious and compassionate, slow to anger and abounding in love, and he relents from sending calamity. God wants our whole heart so He can put His stamp of approval on our lives. That is how we experience better when God says so!

God never stops working on our behalf. When things seem to be at a standstill He is moving something out of our way to get us where we need to be. We wake up in the morning and all our feelings of defeat and fear are removed because God needs us to be still!

Ephesians 3:20; Now unto him that is able to do exceeding abundantly above all that we ask or think, according to the power that worketh in us.

I pray you are encouraged to know that God will hear us no matter where we are. Thank you for purchasing this book. It is available at Amazon.com and Barnes and Noble. You may also contact me by email at shirleygamble@msn.com

Printed in the United States
by Baker & Taylor Publisher Services